Cambridge Young Learners English Tests

Cambridge Movers 6

Examination papers from

University of Cambridge ESOL Examinations:

English for Speakers of Other Languages

CAMBRIDGE
UNIVERSITY PRESS

CAMBRIDGE UNIVERSITY PRESS
Cambridge, New York, Melbourne, Madrid, Cape Town, Singapore, São Paulo, Delhi

Cambridge University Press
The Edinburgh Building, Cambridge CB2 8RU, UK

www.cambridge.org

Information on this title: www.cambridge.org/9780521739368

First published 2009

Printed in Italy by L.E.G.O. S.p.A.

A catalogue record for this publication is available from the British Library

ISBN 978-0-521-73936-8 Student's Book
ISBN 978-0-521-73937-5 Answer Booklet
ISBN 978-0-521-73938-2 Audio CD

Cover design by David Lawton
Produced by HL Studios

Cambridge University Press has no responsibility for the persistence or
accuracy of URLs for external or third-party Internet websites referred to in
this publication, and does not guarantee that any content on such websites is,
or will remain, accurate or appropriate. Information regarding prices, travel
timetables and other factual information given in this work are correct at
the time of first printing but Cambridge University Press does not guarantee
the accuracy of such information thereafter.

<u>Contents</u>

Part 1
— 5 questions —

Listen and draw lines. There is one example.

Peter   Jill   Anna   Sally

Paul   Nick   Mary

Part 2
– 5 questions –

Listen and write. There is one example.

THE BIRTHDAY PARTY

Day:	Saturday	
1	Place:	The .... Café
2	Number of children:	....
3	Where they sat:	table ....
4	Food:	cake, ... and ice cream
5	Drinks:	lemonade and .... juice

Part 3
– 5 questions –

What did John do last week?
Listen and draw a line from the day to the correct picture. There is one example.

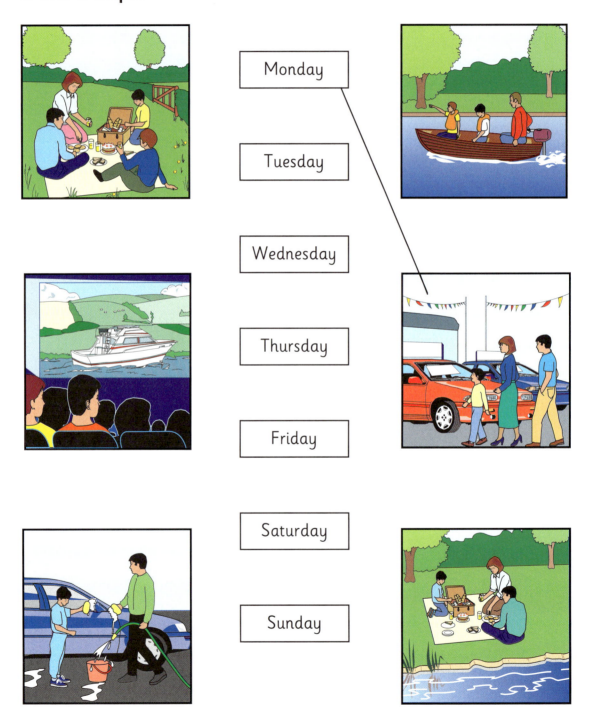

Part 4
– 5 questions –

Listen and tick (✔) the box. There is one example.

What did Sam do at school today?

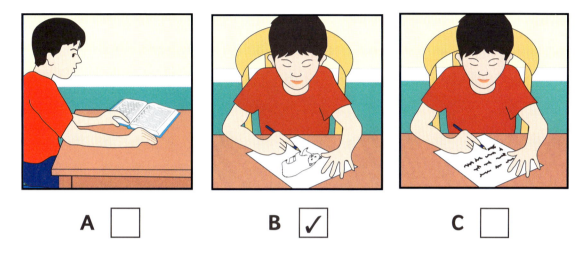

A ☐   B ✔   C ☐

1   What's the matter with Daisy?

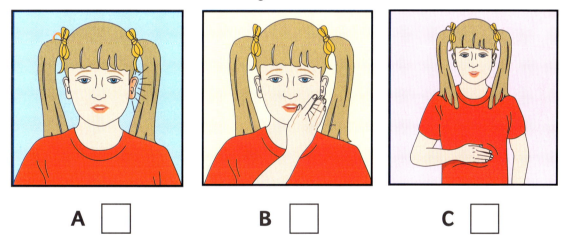

A ☐   B ☐   C ☐

2   Which child is Ben?

A ☐   B ☐   C ☐

7

3   What does John want for lunch?

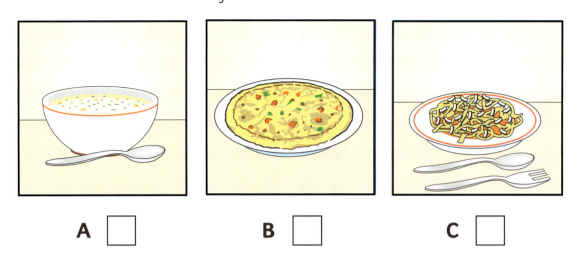

A ☐   B ☐   C ☐

4   What can Jane and Jim do?

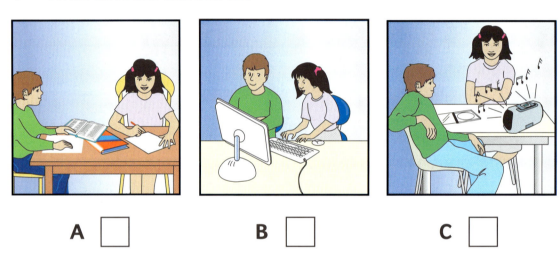

A ☐   B ☐   C ☐

5   What did Nick do at the weekend?

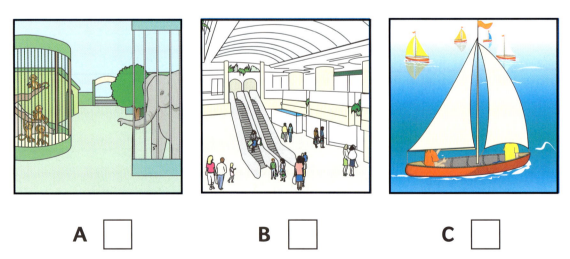

A ☐   B ☐   C ☐

Part 5
– 5 questions –

Listen and colour and draw. There is one example.

9

Reading and Writing

Part 1

– 6 questions –

Look and read. Choose the correct words and write them on the lines. There is one example.

a pen

handbags

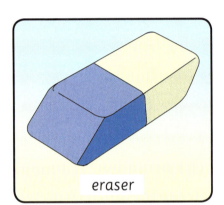

eraser

a rainbow

shoes

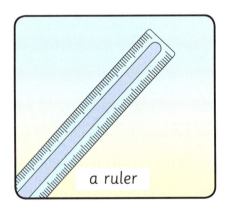

a ruler

a coat

snow

Example

This has numbers on it. You can draw lines with it.

.... *a ruler* ....

Questions

1   This always has seven colours and it is very beautiful.

....

2   This is long and thin. You write with it.

....

3   Women carry these. They put things in them.

....

4   People wear these on their feet.

....

5   Children love playing in this. It's white.

....

6   People wear this in cold weather. It's like a long jacket.

....

Part 2
– 6 questions –

Look and read. Write yes or no.

Examples

It is night in the street.   *yes*
....

There are two plants next to the door.   *no*
....

Questions

1   The young girl is riding the bigger
     horse.   ....

2   The man with a moustache is wearing
     a blue scarf.   ....

3   The woman who is on the horse has
     got a guitar on her back.   ....

4   A snake is going up the tree.   ....

5   There are some glasses under the
     table.   ....

6   The boy on the balcony is laughing.   ....

Part 3
– 6 questions –

Read the text and choose the best answer.

Example

John:	Hello, my name's John. Are you new at this school?

Fred:	A Yes, you do.
	Ⓑ Yes, I am.
	C Yes, he is.

Questions

1	**John:**	When did you start here?

	Fred:	A It was my first day yesterday.
		B I came to learn English.
		C I started my lessons here.

2   **John:**   Have you got any brothers and sisters?

      Fred: A   Yes, we've got some of it.
                                  B   Yes, they've got a big family.
                                  C   Yes, I've got two brothers.

3   **John:**   What's your favourite sport?

      Fred: A   I love football.
                                    B   I play at the weekend.
                                  C   I'd like a game.

4   **John:**   Would you like to play with me on Saturday?

      Fred: A   No, I played baseball.
                                    B   You'd like to play tennis.
                                  C   I've got a swimming lesson.

5   **John:**   How do you come to school?

      Fred: A   To the town.
                                    B   On my bike.
                                  C   After breakfast.

6   **John:**   Can I come with you sometimes?

      Fred: A   Yes, I can come with you.
                                    B   Yes, you went with me.
                                  C   Yes, I'd like that.

Part 4

– 7 questions –

Read the story. Choose a word from the box. Write the correct word next to numbers 1–6. There is one example.

It was Thursday evening. Nick and his mum were in the

..........Kitchen.......... . It was hot and Nick **(1)** .... the

window. Then Mum started to **(2)** ....

the evening meal. She said, "It's fish and chips tonight."

Nick said, "Mum, I don't like fish. Can we have burgers, please?"

"No, sorry. Fish is good for you," she said.

Nick **(3)** .... down to do his homework. Some

of it was very difficult and Mum came to help him. When

she looked round, the fish wasn't there! A cat was at

the window with the fish in its **(4)** ....

When it saw Mum, it jumped down and **(5)** .... to a tree.

There was't any more food in the house. Nick

and his Mum went to a café. Nick had a burger and

salad and a big **(6)** .... He was very happy!

Example

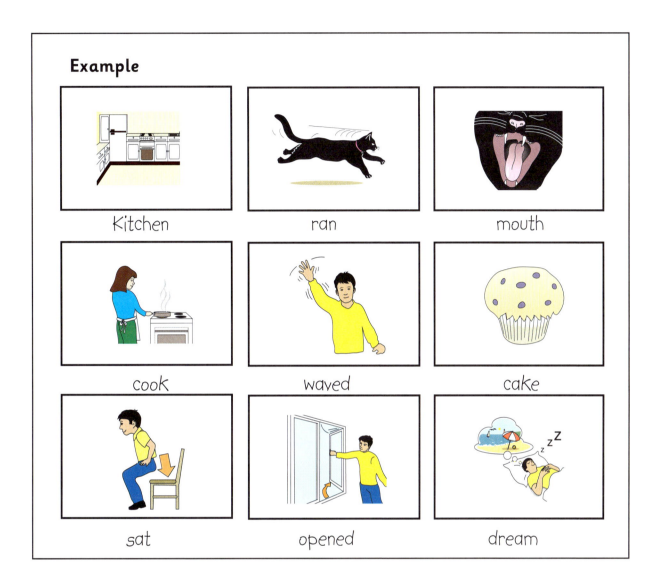

Kitchen   ran   mouth

cook   waved   cake

sat   opened   dream

(7) Now choose the best name for the story.

Tick one box.

Dad helps Mum in the house ☐

A hungry cat takes the fish ☐

Mum and Nick cook burgers ☐

Part 5

– 10 questions –

Look at the pictures and read the story. Write words to complete the sentences about the story. You can use 1, 2 or 3 words.

Grandpa Bill

Last week, Sam and Anna's Grandpa Bill came to their house. They loved days with their grandfather because he did lots of exciting things with them. On Saturday, the children went to the zoo in their grandfather's car. Sam loved the monkeys and Anna loved the lions. At the end of the morning, they wanted to go home again, but Grandpa Bill couldn't start the car.

Examples

Grandpa Bill went to the children's house ....*last week*.............. .

Sam and Anna ....*loved*.............. being with their grandfather.

Questions

1   Grandpa Bill took the children to the zoo on ....

2   At the zoo, Sam liked the .... a lot.

3   When the children wanted to go home, their grandfather couldn't

.... the car.

They ran quickly to the bus station to catch a bus. On the bus, they started talking to two older children, Ben and Alex, who were with their parents. Grandpa Bill told the four children some very funny stories and they laughed a lot.

Then the mother said, "Would you all like to come to our house for lunch? We've got a swimming pool in the garden. You can swim there before lunch." Grandpa Bill said, "Thank you. We'd like that!"

4   Grandpa Bill, Anna and Sam caught a bus at the

       ....

5   The two older children on the bus were called

       ....

6   Grandpa Bill's .... were very funny.

7   The older children's family had a .... in their
       garden.

The family's house was very old. It was big and all the walls were blue. The four children swam then played badminton. Grandpa Bill watched them play. Then for lunch they all had chicken and vegetables. Alex took pictures of the family's three new friends and then Grandpa Bill, Sam and Anna said goodbye and went home.

8   The colour of the family's house was ....

9   The children played .... after their swim.

10 The family and their new friends ate .... for lunch.

Blank Page

Part 6
– 5 questions –

Read the text. Choose the right words and write them on the lines.

Teeth

Example   We have teeth in our mouths. ....They................ are white.

1   We .... our food with them.

Very young babies can't have food like apples, meat or

2   coconuts .... they don't have

any teeth. They drink lots of milk.

Children's first teeth are very small. Then new teeth come.

3   These are bigger and stronger .... the first

4   teeth. You must clean your teeth .... day.

Most people clean their teeth in the morning and at night

5   before they .... to bed.

	It	They	Theirs
Example	It	They	Theirs
1	eat	eats	eating
2	but	or	because
3	that	then	than
4	some	every	all
5	going	go	goes

Part 1

– 5 questions –

Listen and draw lines. There is one example.

Daisy   Fred   Jill   Paul

Mary   Jim   Peter

Part 2

– 5 questions –

Listen and write. There is one example.

MR SNOW'S PARROT

	Colour:	......red and green......
1	Age:	....
2	Favourite food:	....
3	Can say:	....
4	Where it lives:	on................................
5	Name:	....

Part 3
– 5 questions –

What did Sally do last week?
Listen and draw a line from the day to the correct picture. There is one example.

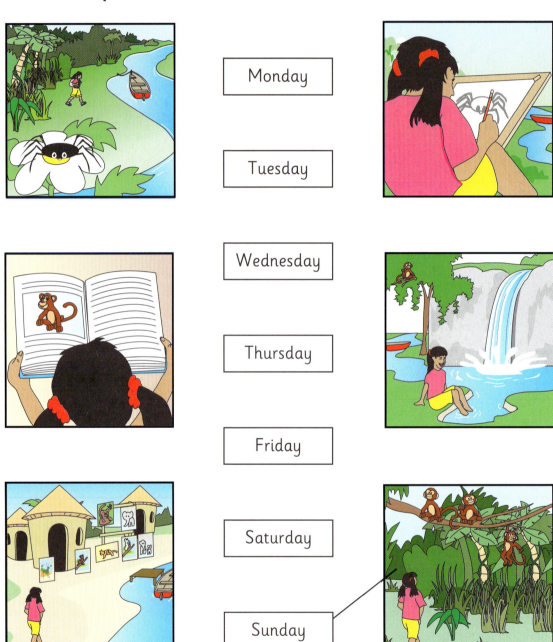

Part 4
– 5 questions –

Listen and tick (✔) the box. There is one example.

Where's Ann's scarf?

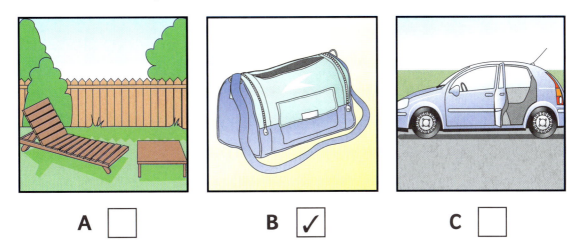

A ☐   B ✓   C ☐

1   What is Nick listening to?

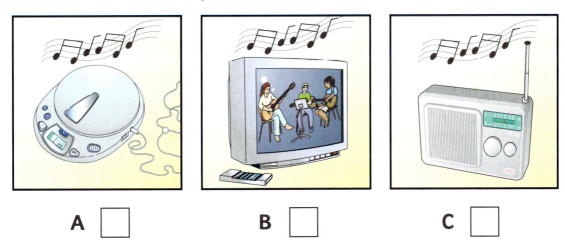

A ☐   B ☐   C ☐

2   Which man is Sue's teacher?

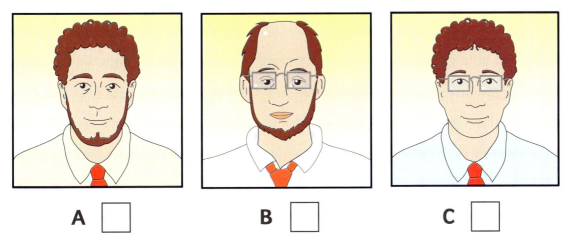

A ☐   B ☐   C ☐

3   What does Pat want to do today?

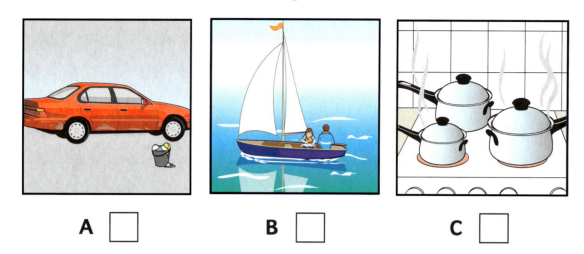

A ☐   B ☐   C ☐

4   Why has Ben got a stomach ache?

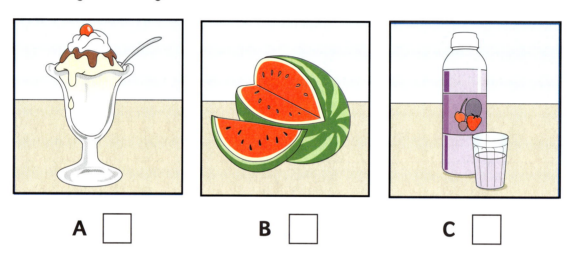

A ☐   B ☐   C ☐

5   What does Bill want to see first at the zoo?

A ☐   B ☐   C ☐

Part 5
– 5 questions –

Listen and colour and draw. There is one example.

Reading and Writing

Part 1

– 6 questions –

Look and read. Choose the correct words and write them on the lines. There is one example.

rabbits

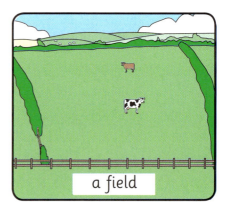

a field

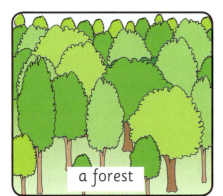

a forest

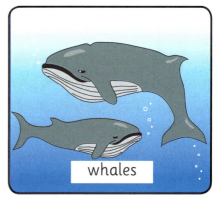

whales

a waterfall

pandas

lions

leaves

Example

You can see cows in this in the countryside.   *a field*
                                                    ....

Questions

1   These are good pets and they like eating carrots.   ....

2   Most of these are green. You see them on plants.   ....

3   These animals are a kind of bear and they are
     black and white.   ....

4   These are big animals which only eat meat.   ....

5   There are always a lot of trees in this place.   ....

6   These animals are the biggest in the world.
     They live in the sea.   ....

Part 2
– 6 questions –

Look and read. Write yes or no.

Examples

There is only one cloud in the picture. .... *yes* ....

Three children are riding on the dolphins. .... *no* ....

Questions

1   The girl in the bigger boat is wearing
    a scarf.   ....

2   One of the children has a jacket
    which is pink.   ....

3   On the island there are two mountains
    with a lake between them.   ....

4   The dog has got a ball in its mouth.   ....

5   The birds are flying above the rock.   ....

6   'Windy Days' is the name of one of
    the boats.   ....

Part 3
– 6 questions –

Read the text and choose the best answer.

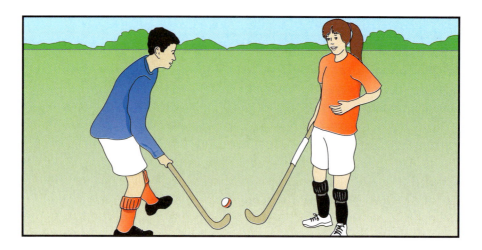

Example

Jane: Hello! How are you?

Peter: Ⓐ I'm very well.
B I'm ten.
C I'm Peter.

Questions

1 **Jane:** Can you play hockey this evening?

Peter: A Yes, I can.
B I like playing.
C You can play.

2 **Jane:** The game starts after school. Is that OK?

   Peter: A He's good.
               B That's fine.
               C This isn't bad.

3 **Peter:** Where is the hockey game?

   Jane: A You hit a small white ball.
              B With my friends.
              C At the Sports Centre.

4 **Peter:** I love playing hockey.

   Jane: A Yes, it's great.
              B Yes, thank you.
              C Yes, it is.

5 **Peter:** Do you like swimming?

   Jane: A Yes, I do.
              B He wants to.
              C You did.

6 **Jane:** Would you like to go to the beach after the game?

   Peter: A Yes, I am.
               B Yes, I would.
               C Yes, I have.

Part 4

– 7 questions –

Read the story. Choose a word from the box. Write the correct word next to numbers 1–6. There is one example.

My family lives in a ....*flat*........... in the city. Last Monday, my younger brother, John, who is eight **(1)**........................... home after school.

"I don't want to go up all those **(2)**..........................," John thought.

"I can climb the big tree in the garden and **(3)**.......................... on to our balcony!"

He carried his school bag on his **(4)**.......................... and climbed up the tree. It was easy!

"Hello Mum, I'm home!" he **(5)**.........................., but there was no answer. The door opened and an old woman came out.

"Oh! Mrs Brown!" said John. "I'm very sorry! I think I'm on the **(6)**.......................... balcony!"

Mrs Brown laughed. "John, you're not a cat," she said. "Why didn't you take the lift?"

"Oh!" said John. "That's boring!"

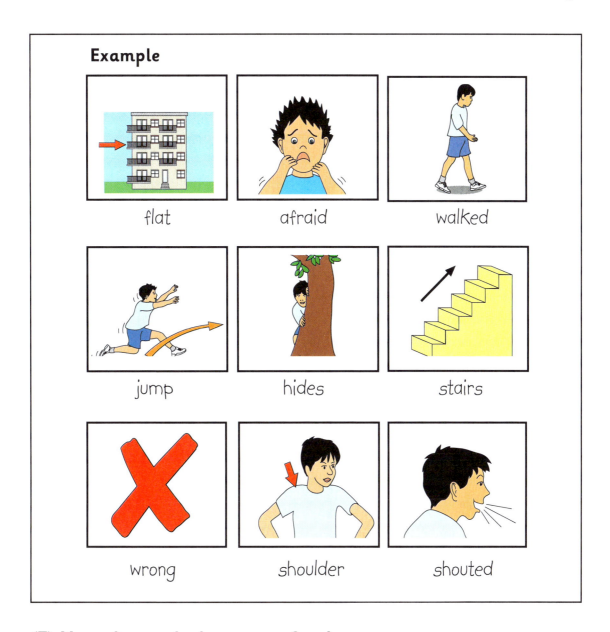

Example

flat	afraid	walked
jump	hides	stairs
wrong	shoulder	shouted

(7) Now choose the best name for the story.

Tick one box.

My brother's funny mistake ☐

John's busy day at school ☐

My family's nice house ☐

Part 5
– 10 questions –

Look at the pictures and read the story. Write words to complete the sentences about the story. You can use 1, 2 or 3 words.

Paul's birthday

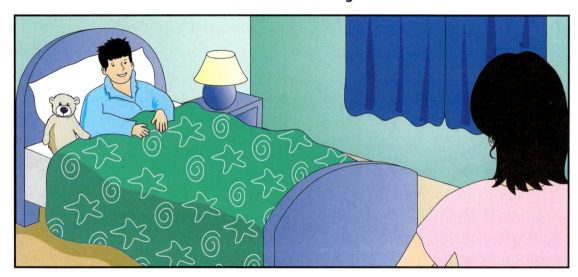

It was Thursday morning. Paul opened his eyes and sat up in bed. "It's my birthday. I'm ten today," he said to his favourite bear. He looked at his old toys in the cupboard opposite his bed. "I don't need those toys now," he said. His mother came into his room with some presents. "Happy Birthday, Paul!" she said. "What do you want to do today? Go to the zoo? The cinema?"

"I don't want to go out," Paul said. "I'm ten now. I must put my old toys in the basement."

"OK," said his mother quietly.

Examples

Paul's birthday was on ......*Thursday*...... .

Paul talked to his ......*favourite bear*...... first.

Questions

1   Paul's old toys were in a cupboard which was

....

2   Paul's .... said "Happy Birthday!"

3   Paul wanted to take his toys downstairs to the

....

After breakfast, they found three boxes which they carried upstairs.
Paul's mum picked up his toy train and put it in the first box.
"No," said Paul. "I like playing with that sometimes."
Then she put Paul's kangaroo very carefully in the second box.
"No," said Paul. "I like his face. He's always smiling."

4   Paul and his mother carried .... upstairs.

5   The first toy that Mum picked up was Paul's

     ....

6   The kangaroo went in the .... box.

7   Paul liked his kangaroo's happy ....

Paul's mum put his kite in the third box.

"No," said Paul. "Dad and I play with that in the park sometimes."

"Dad's toy cars are under our bed, Paul, and he's a lot older than you. You don't need these boxes," said Mum. "How about going to the zoo?"

Paul laughed. "Oh, yes!" he said. "Let's go!"

8   Paul and his father play in .... with Paul's kite sometimes.

9   Paul's father's .... were under the bed.

10   In the end, Paul wanted to go to .... with his mum.

Blank Page

Part 6

– 5 questions –

Read the text. Choose the right words and write them on the lines.

Farms

Example There's a lot of work to do on .... *a* farm. In cold weather, people must give the sheep and cows

1 .... food. Then there are a lot of things and places which people must clean. After that, they

2 .... to work in the fields. At some farms,

3 you can .... vegetables, plants, cheese and beautiful big brown eggs in a shop on the farm.

4 The work on farms .... stops. There are always things to do in sunny weather, in the rain

5 .... in the snow.

Example	any	some	a
1	their	her	its
2	do	can	have
3	buys	buy	buying
4	not	never	nothing
5	but	than	or

Listening

Part 1
– 5 questions –

Listen and draw lines. There is one example.

Paul   Mary   Sally   Jill

Fred   Daisy   Jim

Part 2
– 5 questions –

Listen and write. There is one example.

HOMEWORK – Shopping in town

Favourite shop: .... the supermarket ....

1 Always buys: ....

2 How she goes: by ....

3 Goes with: her ....

4 When she goes: in the ....

5 Name: Mrs ....

Part 3
– 5 questions –

What did Kim do last week?
Listen and draw a line from the day to the correct picture. There is one example.

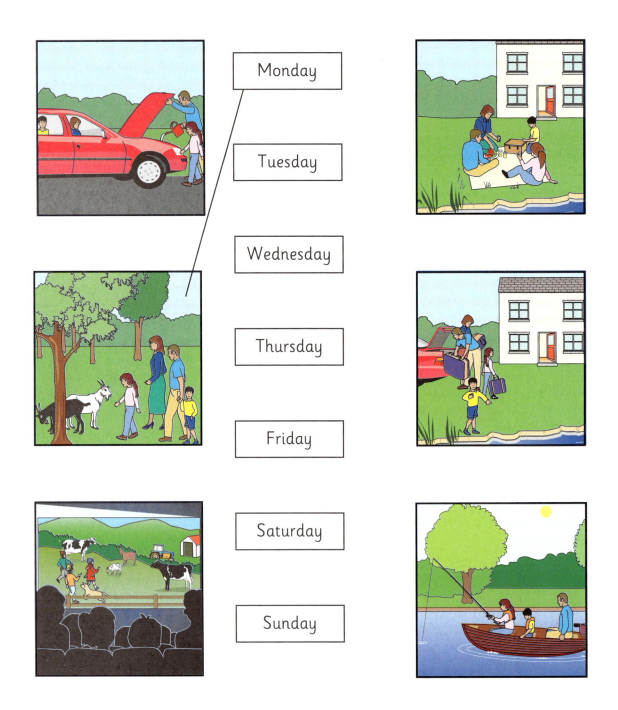

Part 4
– 5 questions –

Listen and tick (✔) the box. There is one example.

What must Jane do first?

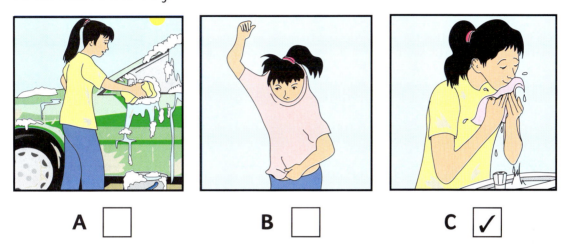

A ☐　　　　**B** ☐　　　　**C** ✓

1　What can the people see outside?

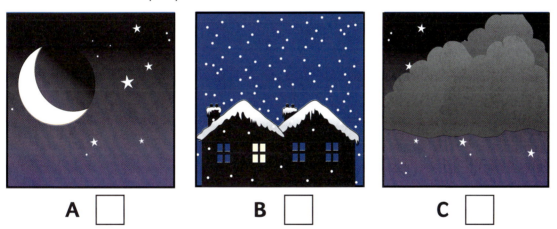

A ☐　　　　**B** ☐　　　　**C** ☐

2　What's the matter with Sally?

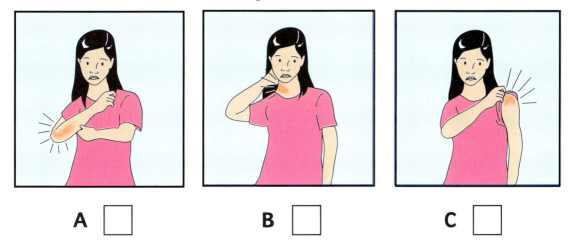

A ☐　　　　**B** ☐　　　　**C** ☐

3   Which picture does the girl like?

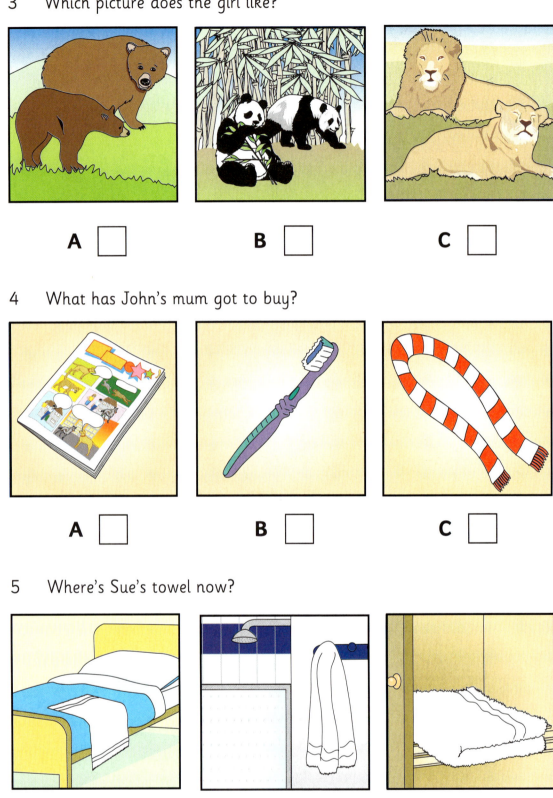

A ☐   B ☐   C ☐

4   What has John's mum got to buy?

A ☐   B ☐   C ☐

5   Where's Sue's towel now?

A ☐   B ☐   C ☐

Part 5
– 5 questions –

Listen and colour and write. There is one example.

Reading and Writing

Part 1
– 6 questions –

Look and read. Choose the correct words and write them on the lines. There is one example.

an island

leaves

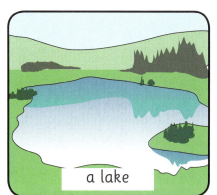

a lake

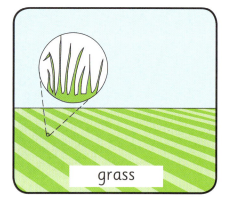

grass

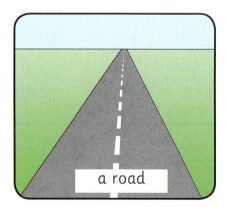

a road

a farm

forests

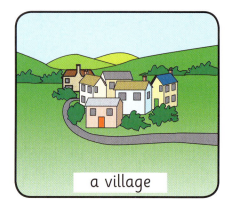

a village

Example

You see this green plant on the ground in
some gardens.

...........grass...........

Questions

1   This is like a small town. There are houses
and people in it.

....

2   There are always a lot of trees in these.

....

3   Boats go on this and fish live in it.

....

4   You see these on most plants and trees.

....

5   Cars, buses and lorries go on this. It is
often grey.

....

6   You have to cross water to go to this place.

....

Part 2
– 6 questions –

Look and read. Write yes or no.

Examples

The man is reading a comic and smiling. .... yes ....

The woman has a towel on her head. .... no ....

Questions

1   The boy who's on the balcony is
    wearing glasses.   ....

2   Inside the apartment, you can see
    a fan between the two lamps.   ....

3   There's a coat on the armchair in
    the living room.   ....

4   There's a black and white rabbit
    under the man's chair.   ....

5   The boy who's waving has curly
    fair hair.   ....

6   Most of the people in the picture
    are sitting down.   ....

Part 3
– 6 questions –

Read the text and choose the best answer.

Jill and her sister, Daisy, are talking about a new girl in Jill's class.

Example

Jill: There was a new girl in our class today.

Daisy: A   Were you?
                        B   Did she?
                        (C) Was there?

Questions

1   **Daisy:**   Is she ten, like you?

     Jill: A   No, she's got nine.
                      B   No, she's younger.
                      C   No, she likes music.

2 **Daisy:**   And what's her name?

  Jill: A   It's Mary, I think.
              B   Mary didn't ask me.
              C   This is Mary.

3 **Daisy:**   Who did she sit with?

  Jill: A   It's on the chair.
              B   All the children were there.
              C   She sat next to me.

4 **Daisy:**   Has she got any brothers or sisters?

  Jill: A   Here they are.
              B   She does a lot.
              C   I don't know.

5 **Daisy:**   Did you play with her in the playground?

  Jill: A   Yes, she's better than her.
              B   Yes, we had a good game.
              C   Yes, I waited there.

6 **Daisy:**   And has she got a bike?

  Jill: A   Yes, we can ride to school with her!
              B   Yes, you're riding them to school.
              C   Yes, he rode it to school before.

Part 4
– 7 questions –

Read the story. Look at the pictures in the box. Write the correct words next to numbers 1–6. There is one example.

Mr Lime loved his work at the zoo.

Every day he .... washed .... the elephants and gave the

(1)........................... and tigers their food, but his favourite animals

were two kangaroos. Every morning, he put some **(2)**...........................

in a big yellow bowl and took it to them. The kangaroos always saw him

and **(3)**........................... to their bowl and ate it all very quickly.

They enjoyed it!

One fine morning, Mr Lime put two big apples in the kangaroos' bowl for

them to eat.

He waited and waited but they didn't come.

"I don't understand this," Mr Lime **(4)**........................... .

"I can't find the kangaroos!" he told the woman who worked in the

zoo **(5)**........................... .

"Oh! They had a new baby yesterday," she said. "Look! They're all sleeping

outside. They're enjoying the hot **(6)**........................... . Now you've

got three favourite animals, Mr Lime, not two!" she laughed.

Example

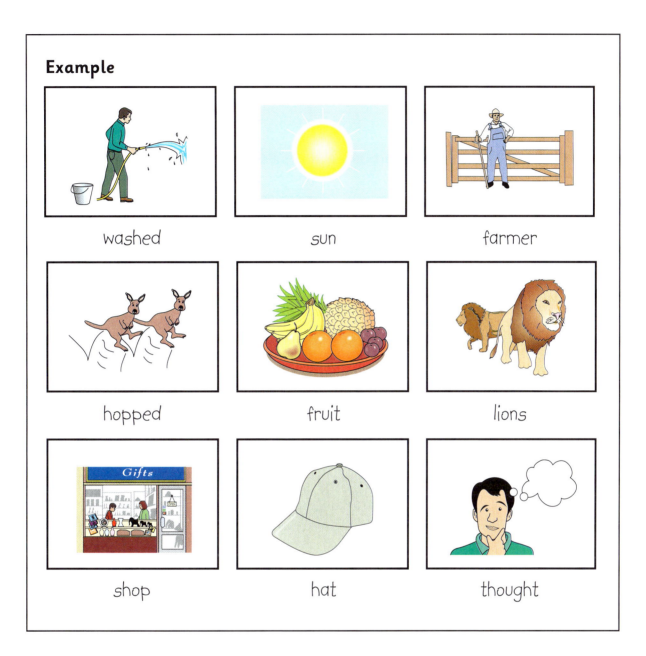

washed   sun   farmer

hopped   fruit   lions

shop   hat   thought

(7) Now choose the best name for the story.

Tick one box.

Mr Lime enjoys his breakfast ☐

A new baby at the zoo ☐

All the animals have a bath ☐

Part 5
– 10 questions –

Look at the pictures and read the story. Write words to complete the sentences about the story. You can use 1, 2 or 3 words.

The Beach

The beach is Peter's favourite place. In sunny weather, he likes going there after school with his best friend, Tony, to swim or to climb on the rocks. On cloudy days, they often play football on the sand there.

Last Saturday morning, Peter woke up and looked outside. The weather wasn't good. It was very windy.

Examples

The place that Peter likes best is .... *the beach* ....

.... *Tony* .... is the name of Peter's best friend.

Questions

1   Peter likes to .... on the rocks or swim.

2   When it's .... , Peter and his friend play

     football on the beach sometimes.

3   When Peter got up in the morning last .... ,

     the weather was bad.

He and his father had breakfast and Peter said, "I can't play football on the beach today, because I can't find my ball. What can I do?"

"We can go and watch the fishing boats," Dad answered. "Go and get our coats. They're in the cupboard."

They put them on and walked down the road to the beach.

"Wow! Look!" said his father. "Something's in the water. Is it a toy boat?"

"It's round. It's not a boat. It's my ball!" Peter answered.

4   Peter had breakfast with .... that morning.

5   Peter's father wanted to go and see ....

6   They put on their .... and then went for a walk to the beach.

7   Peter saw his .... in the sea.

"Tony and I lost it here on Monday evening. We came back on Tuesday morning but we couldn't find it," Peter said.

Peter's dad took off his shoes and socks and put his feet in the water.
"Oh! It's cold," he said.

He picked up the ball and threw it to Peter. It was very wet!

"Now we can play football!" he laughed.

And they did.

8   When Peter was on the beach on .... he lost his ball.

9   Peter's dad put .... in the cold water.

10   The ball that Dad threw was very ....

Blank Page

Part 6

– 5 questions –

Read the text. Choose the right words and write them on the lines.

Tea or coffee?

A lot of people drink tea and coffee. But which plants give us

Example .... *these* .... drinks and why do people like drinking

them?

1 You can only find the tea plant .... hot,

sunny places. For a drink of tea, you must put

2 .... tea leaves with very hot water and you

sometimes add milk or lemon. Some people drink tea in the

3 afternoon because they .... tired.

Then the tea helps them.

4 Some people like coffee .... than tea in the

mornings. They like drinking coffee for breakfast because

5 .... helps them to wake up quickly!

Example	this	them	these
1	in	at	to
2	any	a	some
3	have	are	do
4	most	more	best
5	it	they	he

Blank Page

Find the difference

Story

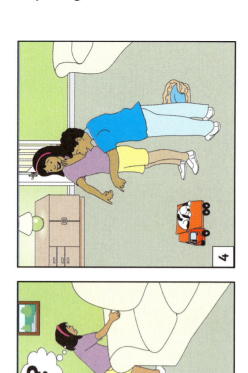

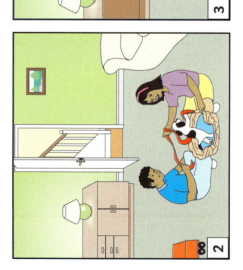

Find the different ones

Blank Page

Speaking

Find the difference

Story

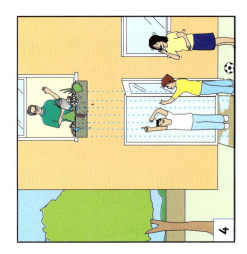

Find the different ones

Blank Page

Speaking

Find the difference

Story

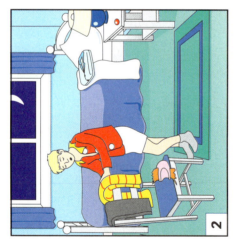

Find the different ones

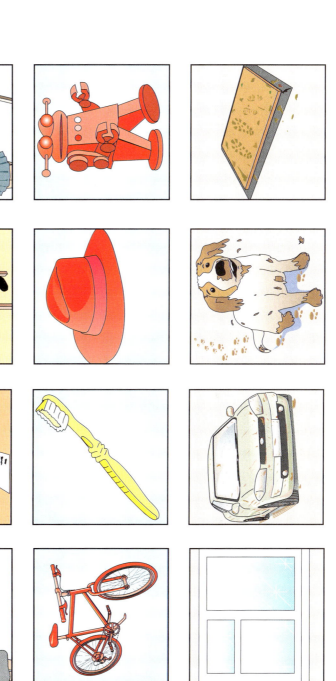